Inspired By Joy: A Memoir.

Jack McGovern

Edited by
Bonnie Botel-Sheppard & Lisa Chavenson

Copyright © 2021 Jack McGovern

All rights reserved. This book or any parts may not be reproduced in any form, electronic, mechanical, photocopy or otherwise, without written permission from the author. For permission requests, write to the publisher, addressed "Attention: Permissions Coordinator."

Owl Publishing, LLC.

717-925-7511
www.owlpublishinghouse.com

ISBN: 978-1-949929-64-5

DEDICATION

This is dedicated to Marion McGovern, who never said no. Without Marion there would be no Jack.

CONTENTS

Acknowledgments	i
Introduction	1
This I Believe: A Secular Epistle	4
Becoming a Teacher	7
Missy	13
Becoming a Learner	19
The Story of Pythagoras	21
The One that Got Away	30
Reflections	35
Surprised by Joy	42
Building Community	45
Everyday Epiphanies	49
Concluding Comments	56
Epilogue	64

ACKNOWLEDGMENTS

"As soon as you walk into the classroom you know that this is a place that respects and admires the work of children. You're likely to see children discussing a favorite author, writing an original play, listening to a teacher share a special book."

- Dr. Helen Oakes

The following pages were written a few days before my 73rd trip around the sun and represent a hodgepodge of memoir and experience. This book encompasses both my experiences and my interpretations of these experiences, which have changed over time. Experiences are lived but then colored by what comes next: the people, the places, and the relationships that create the world we live in. You will meet Missy and Darren, Pythagoras, and Shakespeare; lessons learned, and failures overcome; books that will make you laugh and some that will challenge you to reconsider the power of literature to contribute to a humane and just society.

"Books are the strongest bulwarks against tyranny."
- The End of Your Life Book Club" by Will Schwalbe

This task represents my personal grail quest—setting out to find my purpose in the world. We are all searching for truth to gain a deeper understanding of learning and teaching, and I hope this helps someone find their way through their own teaching journey and to gain some insight through my experiences.

-Jack

INTRODUCTION

Lisa Chavenson

When you meet a magical person, you know. Jack has never realized that about himself, which is part of his magic. There is an energy; a kind magnetic vibe and in its precise, indescribable feeling lies what defines Jack McGovern.

Before I met Jack for the first time, there was a buzz of anticipation in the room where he would join us to lead his annual talk with the Penn Literacy Network faculty. Dr. Jack McGovern walked into the large meeting room with his warm radiant smile. He was dressed in collegiate fashion, holding a leather-bound book – his infamous writer's notebook. These pages hold pearls of wisdom, notes, quotes of meaning to him, rich language worth sharing and bits and pieces that have mattered along his journey.

Some years later, I had the opportunity to work with early childhood educators in Ireland alongside Jack. He has great pride in his Irish heritage. "Pubs and prose, Lisa, that's what we are good at." I can hear him repeat that line with his impish smile and his wife, Marion, giving him a loving eye roll as only a best friend and wife can do. We shared a lot of laughs with family and friends at Temple Bar. His energy and excitement to seek and learn filled the long, tall, imposing corridors of Trinity College's library, a point of destination on his "Places to Visit" list. His excitement was contagious, and he shared what he knew and what he learned that day with all of us.

    I have been in Jack's company for over 20 years and have become a better teacher because of him. Jack is a man of many words (God love him), each precious, wise, filled with humor and care. Mindful and intentional, he is always learning, and we are always learning from him. I thank Jack, my children thank Jack, and my students thank Jack for modeling the importance of a writer's notebook, and for sharing great language, inspired words, good books, things, and people who really matter. His voice resonates with inspiring quotes and great stories. Jack's understanding, compassion, and desire to "do good work" for others has created far-reaching impact in the lives of countless of people. The "Jack effect" will endure and continue to be shared. Thank you, my friend, for inviting us to listen to your stories, to carry those stories and trusting us with your words.

INTRODUCTION

Dr. Bonnie Botel-Sheppard

What can I say about Jack? He is a brother from another mother, he is a colleague, and the dearest of friends. Jack and I met in the early 1980's and our first assignment was to work with a teacher who was written up with negative reviews by the administration. It was during that time, working as a team to support this teacher, that I knew I had met someone who would be part of my life forever.

We went on to teach courses together, create programs for schools in Philadelphia and in Ireland, and Jack became the "Poet Laureate" of The Penn Literacy Network of the University of Pennsylvania, where I currently am the director.

Jack has inspired hundreds of thousands of educators with his wit, good humor, and outstanding stories about the very best teaching and learning that was achievable and meaningful.

Jack impacted a generation of educators looking to humanize their classrooms. This book tells the story of his life as an educator and as a true friend to everyone he met along the way. Enjoy every minute as you read this story about my brother and friend, Jack.

"This I Believe: A Secular Epistle"

by Dr. Jack McGovern

Inspired by Edward R. Murrow, Nikki Giovanni and all the Saints and Scholars who work in our schools.

This I believe:

> That it is hard to grow up and that for some of our children it is getting harder
>
> I believe that our children need to learn that smart is not something you are, but something you can become.
>
> I believe that hope can trump experience and that dreams are more important than some facts.

This I believe:

> That as "Elders of the Tribe" we must listen more closely to the voices of our young and old and those who are suffering, and become strong poets for the commonwealth.
>
> I believe that the best schools are places where, in the words of C.S. Lewis, a student can be "surprised by joy."
>
> I believe our students must be able and passionate learners and that the current "fetish" for assessment can extinguish interest and kill curiosity.

I believe that we need and deserve poetry everyday!

This I believe:

That language is sacred and that every child should be served an extra-large portion of E.B. White, Shakespeare, and Langston Hughes.

I believe that children need Art and Music; the way plants need water and sunlight.

I believe that the nation's greatness lies not in its military might but in the quality of its nursery schools and nursing homes.

I believe that if their life at home is Hell, then school should be like Heaven.

And finally,

I believe that teachers make a difference. They always have and they always will and we should never be afraid of doing well!

This I believe:

That it is hard to grow up and that for some of our children it is getting harder.

BECOMING A TEACHER

"I believe that our children need to learn that smart is not something you are, but something you can become."

I hated school as a kid; my experience taught me that it was a place of fear, frustration, and failure. As I grew, so did my desire to become something more; to create something better for children. Not just for the children, but for myself as well. So, I became a teacher.

Marion and I ran away together to get married when I was 19; she was 18. Marion believed in me, and always believed I could do better with my life. She knew that I had something more to offer, contrary to the evidence. I was always getting into trouble. My mom would say, "What do you want to go to school for? Why don't you get a job at Sears? You'll never be out of work."

After high school, I served in the army. When I returned in 1968, I enrolled in a program called *Veterans in Public Service* (VIPS), which was created by President Lyndon B. Johnson to create opportunities for veterans to contribute to society. About $600,000 was specifically earmarked for training veterans to become teachers, with a focus on inner city classrooms, and I enrolled in that program, not quite sure of what was to come.

On July 30, 1968, some of the veterans involved in this program were invited to the White House Rose Garden. LBJ shook our hands and congratulated us on our service and welcomed us into the VIPS program. The program was set up as a full day training; we went to college for half a day and then spent the other half of each day in a particular school, serving in whatever ways the school determined would benefit the children.

I graduated in 3 years and was finally called by the Philadelphia Board of Education to pick my classroom in December of that year. I chose a 5th and 6th grade classroom at Franklinville Elementary School, which was in North Philadelphia, and was an impoverished neighborhood in the School District of Philadelphia. Franklinville was one of the 10 lowest achieving schools in the district. In education, rarely do low performing schools experience a quick turnaround, and I knew that it would not be an easy path. But

I like a challenge, and I thought this choice would be a challenge for me, and would take my time and my personal investment. In the end, there really wasn't anyone trying to compete with me for the job at Franklinville. Most people in my program chose other schools that didn't have the problems we faced at Franklinville. No one was saying, "get outta my way! I want to go to that school!"

    I knew it would be hard. I was eager for it. Give me the marathon, not the sprint, I thought. It felt like I belonged there, having grown up in a rough neighborhood in Philadelphia as well. My family left our neighborhood in North Philadelphia as soon as I went into the army, which was just after I turned 18. My sister was only ten but had been beaten up a couple times already when my parents left our old neighborhood. They moved into a row house in Philadelphia behind a police station in Kensington and hoped the proximity would protect them from future violence and harm. They were frightened. The neighborhood is safer now, but when they moved at first, it was a rough neighborhood. It's a shame that they didn't have a better choice. Kids need better places to live but we are where we are.

    I called the principal at Franklinville Elementary School to introduce myself and to let him know that I was going to teach there in January. I asked him if I could see the school and meet with him and the children. He said no.

"I'll see you in January after the holidays."

So I waited.

And there I was, in early January, the only person in the building at 7:15am. The principal called me into his office to give me some advice as I began my teaching career. He said, "Son, don't send anyone to the office and keep them quiet." The students had already experienced eight teachers since the beginning of the school year, and I was about to be their ninth. There were 38 students on my roster, but 36 showed up to class. I didn't have an assistant.

So, there I was with my own class. Obviously, the main issue I encountered initially was managing the classroom and student behaviors. It was understandable given their tumultuous school year thus far and the eight teachers who had come and left before I arrived. It was my job to let the students know that I wasn't going anywhere. In addition to managing student behaviors, I also had to learn the classroom systems. The class had 4 different reading groups, I had no idea how hall passes worked, and really wasn't sure how to order the right materials, let alone which *were* the right materials. It took me a couple of months to learn the ropes and get the students settled in. Just like a new parent, I had to learn on the job. My training prepared me for some of it, but there was so much left to learn. The rest of the faculty thought I was a good teacher, mainly because my kids were quiet, and my lines were straight when we walked down the hall. It was really sink or swim at that point.

Around March, I started getting a little disheartened. I followed classroom procedures as directed and used the lessons provided by my principal, which made my class structured and regimented. I was a fine manager, but I wanted to be a teacher, not a manager. To me, this was not really teaching. I was reminded of all the reasons why I hated school as a child, and the things that had contributed to my feelings of resentment. It was not what or who I wanted to be. So, I decided to try something different and plan activities that were not part of the regular teaching program. But the school, especially the principal, felt very rigid, and I knew I had to start slowly.

On Friday afternoons, most of the students watched movies and teachers would take turns supervising the children. It didn't matter what the movie was since everyone was exhausted. There was no learning; just occupied time. And at first, my class watched movies with the other students to give myself time to breathe after a long week in the classroom, and also to fit into the school's culture and schedule. I had to get through the first few months of teaching to learn how to manage a classroom before I was ready to make changes.

The first time that we didn't go to watch the movie,

everything changed. It was a rainy afternoon in Philadelphia and perfect for a movie. It was the kind of afternoon that movies are made for. Of course, when I told my students that we would not be watching the movie there was an audible collective sigh.

"But wait! I think you're going to love this," I remember saying to my 10- and 11-year-old skeptics. They looked at me expectantly, and I took a book out of my bag.

MISSY

"I believe that hope can trump experience and that dreams are more important than some facts."

It started with a book called *"Working with Cardboard Boxes."* At first, it didn't appear to be very inspiring, but it became a catalyst. So, each Friday afternoon, we started to work with cardboard boxes.

I sent a note home to the parents asking them to send extra boxes they had at home. The students started to make giraffes from toothpaste boxes and cars from Jell-O boxes with glue and glitter. They shared their materials, their ideas, and their excitement. They were fully involved. It was a chance to bring creativity into the classroom and get away from the tedium of low-level schoolwork.

In that classroom at Franklinville Elementary, there was one student who stood out. It was hard to stand out among the 38 students, but she did. Her name was Missy, and she came to school about 3 days a week. She was big for her age, and the other children mostly kept away from her. She often smelled of stale urine, and her clothes looked unwashed and dirty. She was obviously neglected and when we reached out to her family, there was never a response. Missy rarely came to school on Friday, but one particular Friday, Missy happened to come to school. When we started building with cardboard, she chose to watch, even though I had an extra box for her in the closet.

"If I bring boxes on Monday, can I make something?" She asked, timidly. Missy always came to school Monday mornings, but she usually left by noon.

"Sure," I replied.

She arrived on Monday with boxes, Christmas wrapping, and paper scraps that her brother helped carry into the classroom.

"Can I make something now?" She asked.

"Yes," I replied, and she went to an area of the room that was separated from the rest of the desks and offered a little privacy. She opened the closet and saw that we had poster paint, unused since my first week at school in January when the custodian told me that children in this school weren't allowed to use paint.

"Can I use this paint too?" Missy asked.

"Of course," I replied. Although they were supposed to be used in art class, paint was rarely used. The art program was mostly comprised of coloring in coloring books.

Missy busily worked throughout the morning lessons. She stayed past noon and didn't even go out for recess. When the students came in, they all started working on their cardboard projects, too, and the activities proceeded in what seemed like an uneventful day. The students enjoyed their time together, creating and sharing as they had done the preceding Friday. That Monday afternoon, the first artistic pieces were created in our classroom.

At 3:00 my world changed.

Missy stepped from behind the cabinet where she had worked all day and said, "It's done."

"Missy," I replied, "why don't you show us what you made?" I was nervous for her to show her work to the class, and in retrospect I know that I could have been kinder to her.

Missy paused, and then from behind the metal cabinet, pulled out the most impressive piece of children's artwork that I have ever seen.

Missy had created a castle. It was made entirely of paper, poster paint, crayons, cellophane, and other scraps. She had made stained glass windows using the paint, crayons, and cellophane. It was breathtaking. Intricate. Delicate. Powerful. The other students were in shock.

"Where did that come from?" one student asked.

The other students in the class started to clap and cheer for Missy. Their applause was so loud and boisterous that other teachers came into my classroom thinking there was a riot. I'm sure it was the first time in Missy's life that she had been celebrated in such a powerful way. And her work was shockingly extraordinary. She smiled proudly, and humbly.

Finally, the class settled down and we put Missy's work on display in the classroom, where it stayed for the rest of the year. From that day on, every time I stepped foot into a classroom and observed children, I thought of Missy and her castle. This shifted my thinking about children, their potential, their hidden gifts, and their possibilities. It changed my thinking about education, and the importance of becoming a teacher instead of a manager, and from a mindset that focused on students' limits to their potential. From stifling to growth. From impossible to possible, and even expected. For Missy, this activity was a lifesaver. Over the next few years, everyone in the school called her "The Artist." She went from unknown and unfriended, to honored and renowned. She was seen. Her gifts had been uncovered.

Franklinville Elementary School was a dilapidated building with crumbling walls and broken windows, and my class started painting murals on the plywood that covered the broken glass. The classroom was noisier and full of energy. My high regard as a skilled teacher eroded, as some of the teachers became disappointed in the energetic and boisterous classroom, and they began to think that I was not as good a teacher as they thought.

"If home is like hell school should be like heaven."

This line represents the mission of my teaching career. It came to me during one of my presentations when a high school teacher asked me, "Really, then, what can we do since the children's homes are like hell?" Without thinking, I answered, "If their homes are like hell their schools should be like heaven." I got booed for that statement a couple of times during presentations. Some teachers saw this as an unwanted responsibility, like I was telling them that it was their job to save children whose parents would or could not. That was not my intention; I wanted to take teachers back to their love for learning that brought them to education in the first place. Were they like me, and wanted to give children a better chance than what they had? Did they grow up loving school and wanting to give that experience to others? Whatever their motivation, I hoped we could all agree that we wanted to improve lives, improve outcomes, and give children – all children – a chance.

Missy did not make it past 18 years old. She was a lonely child living in the inner city with a tough life and surrounded by trauma. I expected to see her work at the Philadelphia Art Museum someday. I hoped she would have the chance to thrive and find her way. But Missy didn't make it. I hope I made a difference with her for the few years when she became known as the school's Artist-In-Residence. Missy had a purpose during those years. Her voice was heard, her talents seen, and possibilities were hers. Although I am sad when I think about her, I am also immensely thankful for her and the way she changed me and the way I saw every child since the day she created her cardboard castle.

BECOMING A LEARNER

"I believe that our children need to learn that smart is not something you are but something you can become."

I was the beneficiary of this kind of thinking when I was stationed at Fort Hood in the 1960's. A local university offered 3 credit courses for $50 to any active-duty serviceman. These experiences gave me confidence and made me feel smarter.

During our first class, our professor passed out the assigned book on American History – a 400-page tome. It should have been called a tomb. There was only five weeks of coursework and the book had over 400 pages to cover – Columbus to Truman.

The professor was right out of central casting – he wore a tweed suit in the middle of the summer. He started class by asking how we were going to read this book, complete all the assignments, and take 3 exams over the 5-week period of the course. A few of us offered up opinions. We would study together. We would work all night if we had to. We would memorize the text. He started to laugh, but not in a mocking way. "I went to Stanford University," he said, "and I couldn't do that. There are better ways to learn."

Over the next 5 weeks, this professor shared several learning strategies and studying techniques that replaced my fear and confusion of learning with success and confidence in my ability to learn.

At the end of the semester, we took the exam, and I earned my first college 'A'. That 'A' felt really good. I felt like I had cracked the code to learn how to "do school" and I was committed to giving my future students the same chance.

I had learned how to learn, and more importantly, I figured out how I learned and what I needed to be successful. It was an epiphany for me, and one that led me to my career in education. How had I gotten all the way through school without realizing how individualized teaching and learning could be, and how to tap into this world. I was engulfed with this new knowledge, and it ignited my passion to focus on how I could help students learn.

THE STORY OF PYTHAGORAS

"I believe that the best schools are places where, in the words of C.S. Lewis, a student can be 'surprised by joy.'"

"I believe our students must be able and passionate learners and that the current "fetish" for assessment can extinguish interest and kill curiosity."

I taught my students how to learn. The lessons from Fort Hood became an integral part of my classroom instruction. One of the challenges I faced was how to use instructional time. You can overdo test preparation and not actually study history, for example. It was a balance. I made this investment in my instructional program. It was worth spending time teaching students strategies and techniques to help them navigate texts.

"Learning is not passive, and students must become reflective learners — not just to the content that they are learning but also to the ways in which they learn and the strengths and needs they bring to the classroom." (Dr. Morton Botel and Lara Paparo, *The Plainer Truths of Teaching, Learning and Literacy,* 2016)

By stepping into the classroom, we have made a covenant with our students that they can become as smart as they want to be. For my students, it started with the return of the Iowa test scores. The reading test was 2 hours long, and students sat silently in the classroom for 2 hours. My class made progress in reading: 75% of the class tested above grade level on the Iowa Reading Test. But for some reason, the math scores wouldn't budge, and stayed significantly below grade level. Not surprisingly, the students also hated math.

I spent many nights brainstorming – what can I do differently? I didn't want to accept failure. My new 5th grade class openly detested math lessons. After I reflected on my instruction and the ways that I was trying to teach students, I realized that we were doing low-level work that wasn't inspiring, motivating, or joyful. The test scores were low, but they gave me an opening to invite a bit of innovation. Why not teach children the powerful ideas from mathematics and see what happens? We couldn't do any worse.

One of the students who I particularly remember from that year was José. One day, he walked over to me during math lesson and fervently said, "I can't do this!" He had given up on his own ability to do math. I knew he was capable, of course, but he lacked the basis for understanding the skills he needed and didn't have the tools to decode the math. It was frustrating for him, and equally as frustrating for me to see a student like José struggle because I knew he could do the work if he felt confidence. That year, I introduced the class to Pythagoras. I wanted a way to help all of the students in my class look for the patterns and intricacies of what made mathematics so significant in the world. I came in with an idea of publishing their discoveries as we explored the beauty of mathematics.

I started by going to a store and asking if I could have some of their discarded wallpaper sample books. These books became our classroom Pythagorean journal. Anytime we were learning math, the students were asked to look for patterns and write the patterns in their own words. These became daily notes as they wrote in their journals throughout the week, and on Fridays I would invite anyone to add their notes to the Pythagoras class journal.

The change was momentous. The students were engaged in intellectual work. The basic math work became our content but the way we approached it was intellectual and engaging. The class journal was our meaning making. It was the students' contributions of our class knowledge that became the fodder to the fire that their learning represented.

I told the students that they were part of a Pythagorean society, and made them aware of what an honor that was. I made a very big deal of the pomp and circumstance of adding to our book, and would ceremonially put on my college graduation robe and invite the students to write their rules in our book of Pythagoras. Our class was learning, growing, and thriving, so much so that they were invited to present at the National Council of Teachers of Mathematics conference in Atlantic City. These were the same children who "couldn't do it."

My students had discovered the joy of cognitive reverie.

I have seen some of my students occasionally over the years as they became adults. One of the letters I received from a former 5th grade student has stood out to me over the years.

"Dear Mr. McGovern,

Are you the same Mr. McGovern that taught 5th grade at Franklinville Elementary School around 1973? If you are, my brother and I were students of yours and you were one of our favorite teachers and we are doing well. He remembers you made books very exciting, and he always looked forward to the next chapter. His favorite book was "Charlie and The Chocolate Factory." I think it inspired him because he is a great storyteller and reader as well.

As for me, I remember I was having trouble with math, and

you had a game called "the bottle game" to help me learn fractions. I remember the pretty colored water bottles and how much fun I had playing the game. It did help me learn fractions. Thanks for being a great teacher. I know you are an asset to the students in Bucks County. Take care and God bless.

- Kathy"

YOLANDA

"I believe that language is sacred and that every child should be served an extra-large portion of E.B. White, Shakespeare, Langston Hughes and Maya Angelou."

One of the great challenges facing children is their lack of cognitive capital. By this, I mean the opportunity to hear rich language, use linguistic tools and read the best variations and interpretations of the English language.

I was convinced that my class needed to have the chance to fall in love with language. I needed a way to excite them about words and decided to have an Elizabethan festival with my fifth-grade students to pique their interest in Shakespeare.

We had to pick a play, and the students selected *Julius Caesar*. I bought 35 paperback copies of the play and told the students stories about Caesar; we read the books and then wrote our own version of the play. We cast the actors. We learned about ancient Rome. This helped build up the students' cognitive capacity and created a baseline of understanding so that they could make sense of the language, the stories, and the context.

Then things got interesting. I told the students about the history of English theater and that men played all the roles. When we went to cast the actors, a girl in my class named Yolanda said, "I don't know why the boys have all the good parts. I want to try out for Julius Caesar." In the end, the students voted to determine who would be cast in the roles, and Yolanda became Julius Caesar by an overwhelming vote. This is what happens when a classroom is safe, and possibilities are welcome.

We took butcherblock paper and created pictures of the city of Rome and discussed how even today there is an enormous effect of the Roman Empire on the world and that without language, information is adrift. How is language informed throughout the world? The intention was to have children learn about the world and the value of language to learn, but in the end, the process became an even more powerful experience for teaching the students about the value that their experiences bring to their classroom learning. They create the glue that holds their understanding together, and each student's glue has a slightly different composition.

It took us about a month to put the scenery together, rehearse and prepare for our production. Then, we needed the audience. We asked the students to invite their parents and grandparents. This was a bit of a gamble, as my experiences with parent conferences at Franklinville had been a disaster. Parents rarely attended conferences and had come to expect that they would only hear about how their children were failing or had problematic behaviors in class. Parents would drop their children off and meet with me. During my first year of teaching, I visited my students' homes to meet their parents because none attended the conferences, and through those meetings had built fragile relationships with some. Because of those visits, or possibly despite them, parents were willing to come to the school and be the audience for our Shakespearean festival.

We had over 90 parents and grandparents who came to watch their children and grandchildren put on a Shakespearean play. This was the first of four annual plays we put on while I was teaching at Franklinville. The parents and grandparents came for their children, but they also came because they trusted me. Those tenuous relationships provided an opportunity for me to show students that I was in their corner, and the parents had a chance to see a positive vision of their children in school in a way that many had not yet experienced.

Yolanda did a wonderful job as Julius Caesar and became a leader in our classroom. She was liked by everyone and had a confidence and maturity that was unusual for her age. Her invitation to learn where her voice held meaning had far reaching implications, and Yolanda grew to become a wonderful teacher as well.

THE ONE THAT GOT AWAY

"I believe that things are hard and getting harder."

During that first year, a new child joined our class. He liked Bruce Lee. He had grown up with trauma and challenges, but he was still just a child in my classroom. I didn't give up, but I just couldn't reach him.

In less time than it takes to throw a baseball from first to second base, half of the students in the class were afraid of Darren. Darren was in his fifth foster home at the age of 10. I met with his social worker, our school counselor, the principal, and his foster mother, and was informed of his early life being a Hobbesian nightmare: short, nasty, and brutish. Darren had been abused, he never met his father, and his mother was on the street. No one had Darren's photograph in their wallet, he had never played a team sport, and he didn't trust anyone.

I went home that night and started to create a plan for Darren so he could make a soft landing in our classroom. When he was nervous, he bit his nails, and he was nervous most of the day. At that point, I had students working in teams throughout the day, and I put him on the aquarium team because I thought they would be the most welcoming and easiest to get along with in the class. In five minutes, Darren had already started an argument with the rest of his team. Not one child in my classroom made friends with him, and they were intimidated by him.

I offered Darren a chance to talk it out, but he refused. I asked him to help me organize the classroom library and, once we started, I asked him about his favorite book or author. Darren said he hated reading. That was understandable because he was two to three years below the 5th grade reading level. One kernel that I did discover was that Darren idolized Bruce Lee, the karate star. So, I went to the library that night, but they didn't have a Bruce Lee book. Then, I went to a local bookstore and found the biography of Bruce Lee. I was thrilled, and thought that this would be the breakthrough that would help me connect with Darren.

The next day, I came to school and presented Darren with the brand new Bruce Lee book. He looked excited to have his own book. He smiled. I told him I would help him read it later in the day during our reading period. I read most of the book to him that day, and he was working hard to read it with me as well, even through his struggle with the language, which was more advanced. I encouraged him to take it home to share with his foster mother.

The next day Darren came to school without his book and said someone had stolen it at home. When I called his foster mother, she said she would check around the house, but she didn't know if he was telling the truth.

I never saw the book again. I told Darren that I would find another copy, but he replied that he didn't like Bruce Lee anyway. He seemed angry at me for even suggesting that he liked Bruce Lee in the first place and scorned my attempts to offer him another book. This pattern of hostility persisted daily for the next three months.

One day, seemingly out of nowhere, Darren went out when the children were painting a mural outside of our classroom. Darren took a glass jar of poster paint and went over to the stairwell as a group of first grade children were coming upstairs with their teacher. He reached over and dropped the jar of paint into the stairwell, where it landed in an explosion of paint and glass. The children and teacher were surprised by the jar of paint. The teacher started yelling and I came over and intervened. Was he curious? Was he trying to get attention? Was he trying to hurt someone in a way that mirrored the hurt he felt? It was impossible to guess, and Darren would not respond to anything we asked.

I felt like I tried everything I knew to do at the time, but I could not reach Darren. He just didn't trust me.

At our next team meeting, Darren's foster mom informed us that she could not continue to keep him because his behavior was disrupting their family.

After that meeting, I never saw Darren at Franklinville School again. I just couldn't reach him. I still feel sad about his experience in my classroom, and regretful that I was not able to make a difference for him during his time with us. He was one of the children who got away. I remember the sadness in Darren's eyes, and I was sad for him. I tried everything I knew just to get him to look me in the face. I fussed over him, I complimented his work, asked me about his interests and smiled at him when I felt that he didn't expect it. Instead of scolding, I joked with him and tried to get him to engage with me, let down his guard, let me in if only a little bit. Darren didn't give one inch. After our meeting, Darren had heard his foster mother discussing his new living arrangements and ran away from home when he learned he was going to be sent away. I later heard that he ended up in jail, which was actually a horrible rumor started by the children in his neighborhood who were intimidated by his anger and resentment. It turned out that after he ran away, Darren went to live with a new foster family in a new neighborhood and tried to establish himself as tougher than some of the other kids in the neighborhood, but it was more self-destructive than powerful. It's as if he thought "nobody likes me, so I'll give you a reason not to like me."

I felt like I made no impact. I had failed him, and I was not the first one in his life to do so. He seemed to hold all the sorrow in the world in his 10-year-old body.

Darren humbled me. Before him I thought I was hot stuff. I could teach anyone. Darren challenged my confidence as a teacher. He didn't care if I was "teacher of the year". To him, I was just one more stupid grownup wasting his time. I had to bring my "A-game" and even then, it didn't matter. I didn't have an "A-game" for him. So, Darren sent me to search for better ways to do school for all children. This reminds me of my mentor, Dr. Morton Botel, who said "we learn more from failures than successes." Darren may have been my best teacher. As Maimonides said, "When the teacher becomes the student, learning happens."

REFLECTIONS

"The poor children of Paris have erased horizons."
- *Victor Hugo, Les Misérables.*

What am I willing to work for? What am I willing to really struggle to achieve? A classroom that's respectful, clean, and orderly? We have kids who need to paint. To draw. To take things apart and figure out how they work. Learning is not always orderly and, for some children, order and quiet doesn't work. Making a mess is an essential part of learning. School is here for the children, and not just for those who want them to stand in straight lines and stay quiet. Taking risks and figuring things out – that is learning.

"When you see something that is not right, not fair, and not just, you have to speak up. You have to say something; you have to do something."

-John Lewis

I agree with John Lewis and his quote above. When you see something is wrong, it is your duty to say something, but also to do something. I felt it was my duty to do something for my students, for Missy, for Darren, for José and Yolanda, and all the students who they represent. For each Missy in our classrooms, how many are we missing in our desire for quiet and order? For many of the children I taught, their lives were full of trauma: grownups who failed them; systems that undermined their potential; people who looked through them and didn't see who they were and what they needed. For all students, and especially for these students, school needed to be different.

When I taught 5th and 6th grade, the children enjoyed the books required by the curriculum, but they were not powerful or moving. Then, one day, I read aloud, "The Outsiders" by S.E. Hinton. Hinton was only 17 when his book was first published, and his writing captivated the students in my class. They were almost falling out of their chairs because this book spoke to their lives. It was about gangs. I'd come in the next day and the kids would say, "Mr. McGovern, please read some more of the 'Siders'." For many of these kids, it was a chance to hear validation about what they knew life to be. It was incredibly important for them to experience this and hear these stories: they spoke to their own lives in a way that showed them that their experiences were important and valuable.

The evolution of my classroom environment over the first two years mimicked my growth as a teacher. I entered a classroom that was uninviting, unclean, disrespectful, and impersonal in a punishing way. It made all the people in it feel unwelcome and like they were not valued.

I flooded my classroom with rich texts that filled three bookcases that I brought in and organized. I brought National Geographic Magazines that were discarded from the library, poetry books, magazines, comic books, picture books, and novels. Every wall and every corner of my room was occupied with literature so no matter where students went in my room, they were surrounded by texts. I wrapped the kids in literature. I surrounded them with words, books, and stories that I hoped would fill their imaginations.

I liked to give the kids lots of breaks during the school day to go and read for 20 minutes, which gave me time to work with small groups. Sometimes, students read to themselves, but many of them chose a book together in a reading groups where the students could support one another. The groups were more like book clubs. I had four or five copies of some of the more popular books like, "Charlie and the Chocolate Factory" and "James and the Giant Peach", for example.

I went to bookstores to plead my case to each owner

or manager to get a good deal so I could have varied texts to work with in my classroom. As a result, students had a choice in what they read, which was incredibly important. One reading group would choose a non-fiction study of an athlete, another would focus on a fiction text. This is the common theme that I followed in my teaching: the value in giving kids a voice and letting them choose. That is the refrain that follows all of this: Missy's cardboard castle, Yolanda's Julius Caesar, Darren's Bruce Lee, José finding his way in math with the rules in the book of Pythagoras. Each of these students experienced their success because of their ability to color outside the lines and make choices for themselves. It allowed them to shine, each in a different way.

 During these early years in my career, I walked around the blocks surrounding the school to see my students and their families, to feel the humming of the community and the landscape of the children's lives. Sometimes I would see something on the street that would be a great addition to the classroom and picked it up, sometimes straight out of the trash. My principal would give me a hard time as I dragged my latest find into my classroom and usually said, "You're not bringing that junk in here!" But often he helped me carry something into the lobby and would ask me, "So, what are you up to now, Jack?" He was a great support to me, and his trust was important, especially as I was dragging trash into his building.

During one of those walks, I found a mantel that someone was throwing away, and I brought it to my classroom. Then, I bought an electric fireplace and set up a corner of my room like a living room with a chair set up alongside. When the kids came in the next day, it was sunny, but I pulled down the shades and they all loved it. It was soul supporting. I sat in the chair, and the students would sit on the floor, and I read to them around the fire.

I convinced my wife, Marion, not only that we needed a new sofa, but also that we should bring our old one into my classroom and set it by the fireplace. My class was located on the 3rd floor of the school, and the cool Philadelphia weather and freezing winters made the room especially cold. The fireplace, sofa, and reading corner created an atmosphere of support and respect for literature that changed the climate of the room. The fireplace and the sofa softened the room in a way that made it a place where children wanted to be and where they wanted to learn. We made it a warmer, gentler, more welcoming classroom. I invited students to learn, to play, to experience, and to explore. I filled the room with games like Monopoly, Chutes and Ladders, and a 50-gallon aquarium that the local minister helped us assemble. My classroom became a children's bookstore and laboratory for learning.

The kids were invited to feel smart.

The students got positive attention and recognition for doing things that were meaningful and praiseworthy. Together, we learned and used the proper scientific names for the fish and the terrarium. The environment was my co-teacher. It gave the children a chance to take responsibility: feeding the fish, cleaning out the terrarium, keeping the game area clean and structured. The students took over the room and they owned it.

The room hummed with creativity and positive energy. The kids felt smart and privileged, and they were proud to be in our classroom. As other teachers visited my room and saw the way that the students thrived they, too, started to bring some of these ideas into their classrooms. We shared ideas, grew from one another's successes and failures, and worked together to bring our classroom communities into the larger school and neighborhood. Professors from local universities visited my classroom and got to know our school. I was making waves, but they were the kind of waves that everyone wants to ride. The changes I brought to my classroom and spread throughout the school activated conversations about policy and paradigms that shifted the way we talked about children and classrooms; about learning and success. This was the seed, planted in my classroom and in many others in Franklinville Elementary School in the

1960s and 70s, and that grew into movements through our district and beyond over the years that we still see evidenced in classrooms today.

SURPRISED BY JOY

"I believe that the best schools are places where, in the words of C.S. Lewis, a student can be 'surprised by joy' and I believe that we need poetry and deserve poetry every day."

A lesson I learned early is that poetry is accessible to all children. Poetry played a significant role in establishing the tone of my classroom. My students loved writing poetry and I offered them a wide range of styles. They wrote haikus, diamante, blank verse, concrete poetry, and a dozen other Franklinville School Originals that they developed on their own. Often, I would end the school day by asking students to write three things about themselves. We called it "Three About Me." Maybe it would be three places they would like to visit, three of their favorite foods, or the three most beautiful people they know (and without many exceptions, they wrote about their grandparents – mostly their grandmothers.)

    We utilized so many formats, and because of that, all the students found one that made them comfortable and feel successful. There was one boy in my class who hated to write, but he created a concrete poem in the shape of a football. Poetry is rich in possibility. Students would read and write poetry for about 45 minutes per week, which was less than I would have liked, but it was what we could do well. I would read poetry aloud so that the children could hear the phrasing of Shel Silverstein, the powerful imagery of Toni Morrison, and the dreams and visions of Langston Hughes, among so many others.

    I published three books of children's poetry each year, and every child in my class had his or her poetry published in at least one of these annual anthologies. We created student-led editorial boards to select which poems would get selected for each edition of our classroom anthology. The board had a rubric to use to help make their selections, and they would look for clarity, originality and the grammar that was connected to the form of the poem the writer had selected. At some point during the year every child had a chance to be published.

    We also chose one student to be our poet laureate for

three months at a time, and their poem was selected for the front page of the anthology. In our room, poetry mattered.

BUILDING COMMUNITY

As I got to know the school and its families, I also became acquainted with others in the community, sometimes through my neighborhood walks, and often through the students themselves. One project that I remember well was building a neighborhood garden in an empty lot at a church in the community. The students began the work, and as neighbors heard about the project, they, too, came to work on it, bringing flowers and seeds to plant. I remember watching families plant together, clean up the garden with their neighbors and other teachers from the school. The minister of the church and families lovingly cared for the garden, and forty years later, it remains a viable space for a garden.

The project began as I spoke with the minister on one of my walks in the neighborhood. What a place for learning. What an opportunity to dig in and show students the impact of their time and attention. A garden is the perfect representation of the work we did together – growing learners and working together to create something great. I had to convince a lot of people that this garden had boundless potential. Not just for what we could grow as a product of our work, but what the work itself would grow. It was a daunting task, and many people doubted that we would get the permissions needed to begin, but once I stopped listening to those telling me that it was not possible, the possible took over. The potential became the focus.

As with almost every other change I made to my classroom, this could have been stopped if I listened to the people telling me that I couldn't do it, and there were many. My internal mantra was "my kids deserve it," and I took it upon myself to convince everyone else that this was what was needed. I had to get past the bullies who said I couldn't do that.

As the students worked in the garden, I worked with them and asked myself questions about the community, and how the school resides as an integral part of the community and neighborhood in which it lives.

- Does the school reflect the neighborhood?
- Does the neighborhood see itself reflected in the school?
- Does the building welcome the community?

- When families walk into the building do, they feel they belong?
- Are the bulletin boards welcoming?
- Whose voices are heard in the lessons? In the hallways? On the playground?
- Whose language is honored?
- Whose stories matter?
- How are these stories woven into the fabric of the community and flow through the veins of the school?

    I feel very strongly that the halls of a school should look like a family's refrigerator with pictures and paintings that reflect the lives and thoughts of our children. They should be proud of the work they see when they enter, and feel that they are valued and represented.

    When the community enters the school, they should see children's original work on the walls that show their individuality and creativity. They should feel that their community and its values are represented

    My experience has shown me the more closely I collaborate with families, the better the students will do. The best classrooms encourage conversations with all their constituents. They recognize the value of the community, cultures, and unique traditions. They find creative ways to involve busy mothers, fathers, and caregivers in their children's education. The schools that provide regular opportunities for sharing cultural diversity are better schools. While I don't have the data to back up that claim, I do have the evidence of my own experiences both in schools that did and schools that didn't, and it makes a difference. From the beginning, my goal has been to give children compelling reasons to learn and grow.

 It's important to think about the context of teaching and learning as we build community. Education and policy are so intent on moving forward that it is easy to miss what's on the sidelines. If the children are not the center of the conversation, they can easily be sidelined and swept up with the changes that policy require. Children need to feel the sense of belonging that is built through the relationships between themselves, their school, and their neighborhood.

EVERYDAY EPIPHANIES

*"A child's time is now. It cannot wait. His body is
being formed and his mind is being formed..."*

The lessons I brought from my early days of teaching are just that: lessons. The value in those lessons is how they inform the work in education that is still yet to come. To know that it happened doesn't make an impact. It makes me feel good to know that I did a few good things and helped some of the children who came through my classroom, but the real potential lies with those whose students remind them of Darren, Missy, Yolanda, and José. How can you build community in your school, with your students' families, and with the teachers around you? Even if you can't lug a sofa up three flights of stairs in the winter, what can you do to make your classroom more inviting, and to inspire a welcoming, gentle feeling for those who enter?

I want to reflect on the people who I met along the way—those who influenced me and who I hope I influenced.

I recall the thousands of children who were a part of my life for these many years as little vignettes—the epiphanies—the magical experiences that caused the seismic shifts in what continually shaped my teaching. These kids have been my teachers, and listening to their voices helps inspired the grit that was necessary to dig in and give them the best teacher that I possibly could be. They deserved nothing less than that from me, and today's students also need champions in each of their teachers. This is not about lesson plans, activities, or even the poster paint that became a mess on the floor. The story has been about those people who made a difference because they were part of my life.

I started my story with Missy because she was my epiphany. An epiphany is a magical moment; a time when everything becomes different. It is a time when you begin to get a different sense of what's right and wrong; what is beautiful and what is ugly. It is a revelation in your life that makes the world look and feel different. There were things that happened before Missy's castle, and things that happened after. Every experience after was impacted by the moment I saw her for who she truly was. Even though Missy was only in my classroom for a few months, her impact on me was phenomenal. My teaching career was different because of

Missy's cardboard castle and students like Darren who taught me to try harder.

Another student in my class was a girl named Aisha. Aisha was one of the most mature 5th graders I met. She took on responsibilities that no child should ever have to, and raised three brothers and sisters while her mother was in jail. She didn't know her father. Aisha often came to school without completing her homework and was quiet. She didn't speak up; didn't tell me what was happening at first. It would have been easy to get upset and assume that she was simply irresponsible, but for Aisha, it was completely the opposite. Beyond the grading, and beyond the lesson planning, knowing your students and learning about them is the work. Sometimes it's hard work, and for Aisha, it was hard to get her to open up to me and share what was going on at home. But that is the work. And Aisha wrote about her life through her poetry, she shared her stories through her writing, and found validation in the stories she chose to read. Authentic stories touch us, and it makes a difference both in reading them and writing them. That's why children need to have a chance to write their stories; not just filling in workbook pages.

Teaching is not an easy career, and often teachers have to take on systems and policies that get in the way of the teaching itself. When teachers experience this, they need to know that this is part of the journey – sticking their necks out for the kids. The word, NO, or encouraging impediments does not hold a space in a classroom of possibilities.

Another student in my class was a boy named Javier: He loved baseball, and his best friend was Ricardo. Ricardo and Javier did everything together, like Chip and Dale. You never saw one without the other. They were tough boys on the exterior, and they liked to be seen as tough guys. But in my class, they were leaders. They laughed, played games, showed kindness to their classmates and used their toughness to empower others. They graduated high school together, and were making their way toward adulthood. When they were 20, Ricardo was killed in a drive-by shooting while at a neighbor's house. Any loss of life is a tragedy, and although I had lost a handful of students to neighborhood violence, this one struck me especially hard. All I could remember was Ricardo and Javier, who were still the best of friends. I reached out to Javier, and we talked about those days in my third-floor classroom and remembered the antics that the two friends enjoyed as ten- and eleven-year-olds. Those memories were important, and they were reminders to both Javier and me of the community that we built. It was an important conversation to me, and it reminded me of the friendships that can be built when there is space in the classroom for antics, laughing, sharing, playing games, and creating art together.

    Yolanda made me question the atmosphere that I created in my classrooms to allow students to speak up and ask for the experiences that they deserve. Before Yolanda, I thought of my classroom as an equal opportunity classroom, but her request made me reevaluate the way that I was articulating our class values and reminded me that I needed to be explicit so that students understand exactly what they are entitled to in their education. I needed to say that they had the right to equal opportunities; to be who they wanted to be and play any role that they wanted in *Julius Caesar* or any other play.

    The manner in which we deliver these meaningful learning experiences is important. If you never bring Shakespeare, or other plays into your classroom, children may not have the same opportunities to find their voices and experiment with their conceptions of themselves and their abilities. As she grew up, Yolanda and her sister became close to my family. They loved to learn. They loved school. Somehow, they were above it all – all the craziness, all the good teachers and the bad teachers. Yolanda was just a kid who found good in everything.

    Yolanda grew up and became a teacher in Hawaii. I don't have a lot of kids that graduated high school let alone college. She's one of the few.

One of the blessings of teaching so many children is that I am filled with their stories and experiences. I am exhilarated by their stories of success, and heartbroken when I think about those who the system disregarded, or who faced additional trauma. I never could put their stories behind me. They were the moments that changed and informed me as a teacher and as a person. Yet, in those places that held tragedy or sorrow or disappointment, progress has been made because there remain people who are doing courageous things; people who care and who want more. Those who thrive are the models, but those who we fail are models, too.

We really need to listen to kids. We need to know what they want, what they want to know, what they want to talk about. I believe children should be recognized for their talents, for their thinking and what they know. I'm not talking about awards and trophies; I am talking about honoring their work. Schools often present awards to students based on the work that they did or celebrating their aptitude in a particular subject area. It's the students who never get the awards at the end of the year who need the most recognition for their accomplishments, however they are earned. The students who receive the most criticism often need the acknowledgement for their success, and the feelings that they get from their success breeds more success. Should we give participation awards to every child who shows up? No, of course not. But when we give children a chance to thrive, there should be a chance for even small victories to be celebrated in a way that uplifts the whole community.

CONCLUDING COMMENTS

    Teachers reach the most students when they allow some manner of choice in their lessons, especially, in my opinion, when that choice allows them to select what they read and what they write about. When the books that they read give meaning to their lives, students have something that excites them.

    When I was growing up, I made my way into the school library occasionally, and chose books that looked interesting to me, but I needed more than the week allotted to get through them. I remember one day when I renewed a small pile of books, sheepishly, the school librarian looked at me kindly and said, "keep these books longer if you need them." She trusted me to bring them back, and she gave me an extra responsibility that felt good, even if it was a small gesture on her part. If she hadn't said that to me; if she didn't trust me to keep the books an extra week, I may have stopped reading altogether.

This story comes at the end of my journey through classrooms, teachers, relationships, and students who have propelled me through my career. What stands out as I view my career in retrospect is that the importance of any story about classrooms and teaching lies in the lives of the children.

It's about John Lewis and Maya Angelou; Shakespeare and Bruce Lee; the Missys and the Darrens; finding ways to bring more humane and student-centered practices to schools that honors their journey and mine.

Through the years, I have collected snippets of books, poems, and photographs and have placed them alongside my own writing in a writer's notebook, which now reflects many years of collecting. I have been a hunter and gatherer of words. Words that struck me, moved me, or that I simply wanted to hold on to. These words and stories were special, and I needed a place to keep them. As I would read, I would look at certain words, sentences or I would listen to a poem or a line from a song, or video, or from a story. I would listen to hear the language that moved me in a way that made me think, or feel, or remember. Words and poems from philosophers, Nobel Laureates, children, or from everyday conversations. And so, when I wanted to write something, I could look in my writer's notebook and find something that inspired me. When I read the passages in it, I remember how it felt to hear the words for the first time. Sometimes I can even remember where I was, or what the room smelled like, or what colors were in the sunset that evening. Often, it gives me ideas for future writing, or reminds me of something I want to share with a friend or group of teachers.

Before I had this notebook, I wrote these words on pieces of paper, and on the backs of books. I was losing the words that I meant to capture. The slips of paper were pieces but not a whole space to hold the language the way I needed. One day, a former student who had noticed what I was doing gave me a writer's notebook as a gift. The gift was life changing: a place to hold all these words together. Without my writer's notebook, I would have lost so many of these words and reminders. Through the years, I have collected language and I have shared language, some more poignant than others, but all an important part of the fabric that makes up my philosophy about life.

I took the best pages from the best writing that I could find from all the pieces of notebooks, and I put them in this new notebook. This is a place to find the good language again when I needed it. I have filled it with the best writing that I could find. I also filled it with some important photographs, student writing, words of my children and grandchildren, and art.

I like the term hunter and gatherer because that is

how I feel when I'm reading a poem by Shel Silverstein or *Jude the Obscure* by Thomas Hardy, I'm looking for the best art that a human can produce, the best writing that I can find and by holding onto the text it also elevates it and brings it into my world. That's the hunter and gatherer part of this; my passion and pursuit for good language. Below are some of the quotes I want to share, and the words are directly out of my notebook as I wrote them.

"Fairy tales are necessary not for students to know that dragons exist but to know that they can be defeated."

— GK Chesterton

"I teach my students to be friends of knowledge and I teach my teachers to be friends of students."

— Wu

"Falling in love with words. You'll feel the power of a community that allows and encourages life-long learning in science, social studies, and math and in the words of Bertrand Russell teachers "rouse and stimulate a love of mental adventure."

"The greatest danger for most of us is not that our aim is too high, and we are missing it, but that it is too low, and we reach it."

Michelangelo

"Possibilities are the leitmotif of this opera."

-Unknown

"Teach so as to build a child's curiosity of the world by creating learning situations that matter to think about, time to experiment and time to make sense of what is observed. Foster a community where students' and adults'

ideas are respected. Children have a right to expect this in school and in their homes."

- Eleanor Duckworth
"The Having of Wonderful Ideas"

"If you want to build a ship don't drum up the people to gather wood, divide the work, and give orders. Instead, teach them to yearn for the vast and endless sea."

- Antoine de Saint-Exupery
"The Little Prince"

"Reading makes possible joyful communities for endless hope and wonder."

- Yaya Yuan

"Dare we disturb the universe."

- T.S. Elliot

"There was a child went forth every day, the first object he looked upon and received himself, with wonder or pity or love or dread, that object he became."

- Walt Whitman

That's it; those words by Whitman sum up the story of my career as an educator. In fewer than 30 words, Whitman creates a narrative about how children become who they are. It's like a refrain, a statement on how children develop into what we give them or deny them, and yet how each day begins anew, with another opportunity to create a fresh beginning for each child. It's the child; each one, individually, and the potential that each day, each lesson, each teacher holds.

What do kids see of their futures?

When children walk into my classroom they might see a classroom, some books, a smiling face, but within it lies their future and their possibilities. How do you know that you love something if you never know that it exists? How can you learn about someone who had experiences like yours without opening the book where they share their life? It is imperative that teachers learn about each child in their care, as much as they can: what they love, what matters to them. And through this, guide them to see their futures and possibilities beyond the classroom. Children can be playwrights, welders, inventors, artists, activists, magicians – a myriad of possibilities and opportunities just waiting for them to choose.

The students who taught me found their own varied paths along their life's journeys. Yolanda became a teacher. José built his confidence in math and became baseball statistician. Juan is a police officer and protects the neighborhood he and Ricardo called home. Darren found his calling with electronics and found the safety and kindness he was always lacking in his life lay within him. And Missy found her cardboard castle.

The library that welcomed me and trusted me with its books was a safe place when I was a child. It introduced me to stories that I could read for hours. It was a safe place where I could go without anyone bothering me, and without anyone fighting. The library gave me sanctuary. It allowed me to find my safe place, and, without it, things would have been very different for me.

Through my career, I've often been asked to diagnose the needs of a school, a classroom, a teacher. Some believe that there needs to be more testing, or preparation for testing. During one of these conversations, I was asked "Jack, what do children need more of?" I replied, "children need more dragons, unicorns and castles." That means they need more creativity, more communal work, more exciting encouragement. I want teachers to think about their students and pay attention to children.

When I started teaching, I wasn't sure what I was doing. I didn't have positive experiences that pushed me to empower kids. I was going to be a track coach because I loved track. But in the end, the reason why I ended up in that third-floor classroom doesn't matter. The fact that I ended up there, regardless of how I made it, put me in the position to learn about kids, and from them. Through their eyes, I realized that there was more to school than just surviving. There was more to school than the worksheets and lesson plans. It was not just what my students learned from the class lessons for any particular day, but it was their nourishing source of where it would take them tomorrow. I tried to nurture their dreams. Did they see it too? Maybe. But often, teaching is a long game, and children see their experiences in a retrospective mountain – and the ones that make a difference are often buried at its foundation. Maybe they recognized my passion, maybe they remember the moment they realized something about themselves through a book. Maybe it just became a part of the puzzle that makes them who they became. And that, truly, is the most important thing that it could become.

The absence of that is the diminished life that Victor Hugo describes – a life of diminished horizons. And what a tragedy to lose those children. Some of those children will have the answer to important questions, or will break world records, and some of them are just going to show up and be good dads and go to their kid's ball games. They will have fulfilled lives regardless how.

And the stories, his stories, their stories, continue to be shared…

Jack at the age of 8.

To John McGovern
With best wishes,

June 30, 1968 *Veterans in Public Service* (VIPS) ceremony at the White House Rose Garden with President Lyndon B. Johnson.

Jack in basic training for the army.

Jack's family celebrating his graduation in 1978 as he earned his doctorate.

Jack McGovern
Head of School

"It's never too late to have a happy childhood."

From the yearbook of Plymouth Meeting Friends School, where Jack worked as the Head of School.

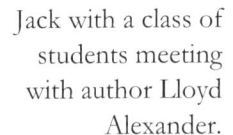

Jack with a class of students meeting with author Lloyd Alexander.

Jack at his desk at Plymouth Meeting Friends School.

Reading to a class of students at Plymouth Meeting Friends School.

Jack (left) running in a race in 1978.

Jack reading to his granddaughter

Inspired by Joy

Entertaining students and staff at Plymouth Meeting Friends School.

Jack teaching a class for teachers.

Jack with colleagues from the Penn Literacy Network, Dr. Morton Botel, Joe Ginotti and Tom Strandwitz.

Epilogue:

By Dr. Helen Oakes, Excerpted from *The Oakes Newsletter*

In 1981, Dr. Jack McGovern was selected to receive the Rose Lindenbaum Award that was given annually to ten of the School District [of Philadelphia]'s most outstanding teachers. A visit to Jack McGovern's fourth grade classroom quickly reveals why he was chosen.

Dr. McGovern believes that his students can and will learn. Without regard to previous levels of achievement, or ethnic, or economic background, he has high expectations for his students. He believes they can be stimulated, challenged, encouraged, and coached to achieve more.

Because many of Dr. McGovern's students lack a good self-image, they must be encouraged to believe in and feel good about themselves so that they may advance and blossom academically. Jack McGovern is always looking for ways for children to taste success and receive recognition. He is quick to praise good work of every kind – a thoughtful answer, the meaning of a difficult work, a creative solution, or a kindness to another child. He creates opportunities for children to "a moment in the sun." For example, during a sharing time, he was fascinated and amazed by the pretty flower that one girl had folded from paper. He was pleased with the poems that another child had written and illustrated, and he had them posted. Each child was made to feel good as s/he shared something with the class.

Jack McGovern is a Vietnam era Veteran, drafted at 18, who came back to Philadelphia and went to night school at Temple University. He worked first as a non-teaching assistant and later as a teacher, He secured his B.A. degree in 2½ years and over the next 8½ years he received his M.A. and Ph.D.

Jack McGovern deserved to be honored as an exceptionally fine teacher. The students who have the good fortune to be in his classroom spend a year with a teacher who cares deeply about them and believes strongly in their potential. They associate with a person who helps them to know, learn from, and admire some of the great thinkers who have contributed to our knowledge culture and value. They improve their ability to speak, read, write, and compute in a meaningful context with much of this learning embedded in the humanities and science. Their classroom life is rich in experiences of all kinds as their teacher shares with them his broad, varied background of knowledge and interests.

Jack McGovern has a doctorate in children's literature. He believes that part of becoming a fulfilled human being is experiencing the joy of reading. He wants his students to know that in books they can find adventure, mystery, beauty, information, insight, escape, knowledge, and challenge.

John McGovern's classroom, both in its physical layout and the daily schedule, reflects his enthusiasm for books and reading. There are books all around the room. He strives to "wrap" his students in them. Many are displayed, front covers showing, on several six feet tall sloping racks that he made himself. At one end of the room, there is a "fire-place" where children can go to read in a cozy atmosphere. The fireplace has a mantle that Dr. McGovern found on trash day, re-painted, and put up. Under it are logs with a light that makes them appear to be burning.

The Value and Fun of Reading

Reading plays a very important role in his classroom. Besides the reading found in most classrooms that occurs in reading groups using a publisher's series of books, John McGovern reads to his students one or more times every day. He believes they deserve to hear good literature and was just finishing E.B. White's Charlotte's Web when I was there. Time is also set aside every day for children to read silently to themselves. A sign on the classroom door bars interruptions. For a period of time, everybody in the room reads a book. A child in Dr. McGovern's classroom comes to know the value, importance, and pleasure of reading. This was in the Sunday times book review, David Byrnes said, "sharing books is like sharing food."

Jack McGovern uses science and other subjects to give students opportunities to write. When I visited it was Day 3 of an experiment involving the germination of a large seed. Dr. McGovern drew from the students and wrote on the blackboard a description of what they had done to date. Each student had a baby food jar which became a Germination Chamber when s/he placed water, a paper towel, and two lima been seeds in it. Dr. McGovern asked them to copy what they had composed together and then look at their own seeds and record their observations. Writing under such circumstances has purpose because students came to see that their records enable them to know exactly what steps the seed went through as it developed a root and a sprout.

Jack McGovern teaches mathematics in different ways. He uses concrete materials, drill, through provoking problems and science experiments too. One morning, the students worked with wood rods of different lengths. There were ten different sizes and colors corresponding to lengths from 1 through 10 centimeters. The children worked with problems such as "find the rod that is the size of two whites." After a time, Dr. McGovern held up a meter stick and asked the children to estimate how many orange rods (10 centimeters) there are in a meter. Their estimates ranged from the correct answer that is 10 to 24. Having attempted to make an estimate, each youngster had his interest aroused and should have less difficulty remembering that there are 100 centimeters in a meter. Each child traced his hand and spread to its fullest, measured the length of each finger and the span. 15 centimeters will mean something to them because they now associate it with the span of their hands.

Another morning the students practiced their number facts by solving three place addition and subtraction problems as fast as possible. Also, there were problems for extra credit that utilized high order thinking skills.

A couple of weeks ago, Jack McGovern took his class to the park to fly a rocket. They tested the rocket with increasing the milliliters of "fuel" and measured the number of meters it flew each time. They pondered the question of why, after a certain point, more fuel reduced the length of the flight. When they returned to class, they graphed their results. Five of the students made a four-panel display chronicling the experience. It was complete with compositions about the experiment and Isaac Newton's Laws of Motion, a graph, and charming crayon drawings of the child in the park.

Clearly, science is taught for many reasons. It stimulates interest, teaches children to think in a scientific way, helps them to learn and to use reference books, provides students with necessary information, and enhances the teaching of the three R's.

A tour of Dr. McGovern's room tells more about life in his classroom. There are two scrapbooks made from discarded wallpaper sample books that provide heavy paper to mount on. One scrapbook is titled "Pythagorean Society and has a wonderful Cark Sandburg poem, "Arithmetic" on the first page. The scrapbook contains rules that children have discovered for themselves about mathematics.

The Rachel Carson Nature Museum has a prominent spot in the room. A plastic case that was used to hold watches in a store now displays a shell exhibit. At other times during the year, it houses fossils, rocks or other items drawn from nature. The children know of Rachel Carson and her deep concern for preserving our natural heritage. They are reminded of her and what she stood for by their museum.

Rose Lindenbaum

Jack McGovern is one of forty, soon to be fifty, Philadelphia teachers honored with the Rose Lindenbaum Award. Miss Rose Lindenbaum is a remarkable woman who devoted her life to the school children of Philadelphia. She began as a special education teacher in 1929, became a Vice Principal in 1959 and retired in 1972. During the last nine years of her career, she worked as a supervisor on an individual basis with failing special education teachers helping them to become successful.

During this period, Miss Lindenbaum decided that she would like to do more to help teachers improve and to reward excellence. That prompted her, before her retirement, to decide to will funds to the School District to make annual awards to outstanding teachers. After she retired and inherited money, she decided that she could live comfortably even if she gave $100,000 during her lifetime to the Board of Education to establish a trust to provide the awards. She made this very generous gift in June 1977.

Since the spring of 1979, ten teachers have been selected each year. Principals nominate teacher(s) from their school. District superintendents, depending on the district's size, reduce the number from their district to two or three retired teachers picked annually by the Philadelphia Public School Retired Employees Association, narrow the list down to ten from the 18 or 19 submitted to them. Seven are to be teachers of regular children and three are to be teachers of special education children. Teachers must be selected on the basis of the following criteria. They "must have completed at least seven years of teaching, possess genuine love and interest in the welfare of children, be dedicated to the teaching profession, possess ability to produce results in the classroom, be creative and seek to grow professionally" and "possess high moral, intellectual, and social integrity."

The Rose Lindenbaum Awards are usually given at the Home and School Council Dinner in May. Each of the ten teachers is presented with an engraved citation giving the reasons s/he is being honored, and a check represents one-tenth of the income of the Trust for that year.

Given Miss Lindenbaum's financial circumstances, her gift to the School District represented a significant sacrifice and measure of importance she places on acknowledging and awarding excellence. She believes that showing appreciation to teachers will "boost teacher morale…tend to lift the image of the teaching profession," and "create an incentive…to work harder to prove the quality of education in the classroom."

Rose Lindenbaum's gift helps to create a climate in which talented teachers can flourish. It stimulates and inspires teachers to work hard and strive to achieve their very best. Her gift enables the School District to identify models of fine teaching, like Dr. Jack McGovern, and to search out and reward the best practitioners of the art. Each year, the School District can stress the fact that excellence in teaching is desirable, appreciated, recognized, and rewarded.

Dr. Jack McGovern uses wallpaper and newspaper to teach Contemporary History in his Alternative Learning Class at the "Franklinville School" in Philadelphia. Sound crazy? His students don't think so. They are totally involved in the subject of current history because they use the newspaper in their classroom.

Let's first explain the wallpaper part of Dr. McGovern's Contemporary History Program. His sixth-grade class is currently compiling a history book, and Dr. McGovern, using any inexpensive materials that he can get his hands on, has "recycled" an old wallpaper sample book for the students to paste their articles in. The used wallpaper book provides a colorful and delightful background on which the students can paste and save articles that interest them.

During this current school year, the students at "Franklinville School" are following three major themes in the news-- the crisis in Iran, the invasion in Afghanistan, and the spiraling price of gold.

The students clip articles from The Bulletin that explain the conflicts, the causes and effects, and the potential, long-range implications of each of these themes.

This kind of editorial exercise reinforces several important kinds of basic learning skills. Reading skills, of course, are emphasized in a highly motivational way. Kids love to read and learn about current happenings that directly impact their lives. Evaluative skills are also practiced. Students learn the criteria for deciding the relative importance of things by evaluating newspaper articles. They decide which ones highlight that point out the greatest significance relating to an important news theme such as the crisis in Iran. Perhaps, most importantly, students practice decision-making skills while learning more about the world in which they live.

Jack McGovern has many different kinds of newspaper activities going on in his class in addition to the Contemporary History project. He has, for example, a "News Tree," which is a learning center to which students can go during the time block set aside for independent activities.

The "News Tree," which literally looks like a tree contains various "branches" with different kinds of stimulation games. The "Who Am I?" game, for example, involves having students match faces and names of people in the news. Both the faces and the names are glued on separate round cardboard discs. An answer key is provided with the game so that students can independently evaluate their own progress.

The "News Tree" also contains a headline matching game that involves having students read a news article that has had its headline cut off. The object of the game is to match the story with the appropriate headline. Copies of the original articles with the proper headline are included for students to check their own work.

Another branch of the tree includes a "Cartoon Center" where students learn to draw political cartoons.

The Alternative I class is part of "Learning Unlimited" -- one of the School District of Philadelphia's first elementary school alternative programs. Under the direction of Dr. Jack McGovern, who is described by his principal as "outstanding, creative...a most unusual teacher," the program gained national recognition. Dr. McGovern, a Vietnam era veteran, received his doctoral degree from Temple University in 1971, with a concentration in children's literature. He summarizes his interest in using the newspaper in his classroom by saying that "history is a living subject, and the newspaper offers students the chance to reflect on that living history in a way that television cannot provide."

"Franklinville School" is an exciting place for students. They learn about current events in an interesting and challenging way by using the newspaper in their class with a little ingenuity and some wallpaper. He creates opportunities for children to "a moment in the sun."

ABOUT THE AUTHOR

Jack McGovern is a well-loved, and well-respected educator, a proud Irishman, proud veteran, husband, father, grandfather, great-grandfather, treasured friend, hunter and gatherer of words, sharer of good language and meaningful literature, master of The Writer's Notebook, teller of stories and magician who inspires endless possibilities.

Made in United States
Orlando, FL
23 April 2022